undivided
MARRIAGE

WHEN TWO PEOPLE
BECOME ONE FLESH

Mitchell & Rhonda Owens

Undivided Marriage: When Two People Become One Flesh
Mitchell and Rhonda Owens
©2016 Mitchell and Rhonda Owens

Table of Contents

Welcome

RELATIONAL NOVELTY FUELED BY INFATUATION and chemistry initially magnetizes the connection between two people. Author Gary Thomas calls this phenomenon "artificial intimacy."

"Artificial intimacy begins with the onset of infatuation, a 'grab your brains with a vengeance' neurochemical reaction that makes us virtually blind to our partner's faults but is notoriously short lived with a shelf life of about 12 to 18 months." When the relational novelty wears off, the 'neurochemical' reaction wanes—and that's when problems arise.

Oneness—in any aspect of a marriage—is simply not something that is going to "just happen." Initially, a couple may *feel* as if they are "one flesh" without much energy expended—a result of all that neurochemical connection. But chances are that those euphoric feelings will pass. After all, it is the nature of our feelings to flutter fickly about without warning.

Because no one aspires to "artificial intimacy," the logical next question is this: How can couples achieve authentic intimacy? What leads to a man and a woman living an *undivided* married life where *TWO people become ONE flesh*?

Gary Thomas inspires hope on the subject when he says, "True intimacy—that sense of 'oneness' that we all seek—has to be pursued and built rather than simply discovered and felt."

To that end, we offer *Undivided Marriage: When TWO People Become ONE Flesh*—a simple devotional geared toward helping couples pursue and build the kind of Biblical oneness God had in mind when designing the gift of marriage.

Overview

FROM THE VERY BEGINNING OF THE BIBLE, God established his intent for marriage – that a man and a woman "become one flesh." (Genesis 2:24) Throughout scripture this model for marriage is reinforced, and in Mark 10:8, Jesus makes it clear that when a couple enters into a marriage covenant "they are no longer two, but one flesh."

Whether you've just recently walked down the aisle or have been together 30 years, *Undivided Marriage* is a devotional written to open lines of communication in ten key areas — areas that, without careful attention, may gradually cause slow relational division over time.

EACH LESSON IS BROKEN INTO FOUR SECTIONS:

 THE PROPOSAL: God's proposal to live as one in each area of our marriage

 THE EXAMPLE: Wisdom and tools to succeed in our marriage

ONE-ON-ONE: Questions to identify areas of clarity in our marriage

 DATE NIGHT: Action plans to implement the lesson

When working through *Undivided Marriage* the best schedule really depends on what works for you as a couple. One possible scenario could be as follows:

SUNDAY: Read "The Proposal" and "The Example" sections. Begin working on memorizing the key verse(s) for that particular week and discuss your initial thoughts and impressions.

MONDAY/TUESDAY: Think about and answer the questions in the "One-on-One" section, and perhaps write your answers in a journal or record them on your phone.

WEDNESDAY: Discuss and communicate openly with your spouse your responses to the "One-on-One" questions.

FRIDAY/SATURDAY: It's "Date Night" time! Be as diligent as possible to set aside special time with your spouse so you can not only enjoy time together, but also so you can begin to apply lessons learned from your study of becoming "one flesh" in each of the specific relational areas covered in the book.

Lesson One:
Spiritual Oneness

Key Verse

Didn't the Lord make you one with your wife?
In body and spirit you are his.
~Malachi 2:15 (NLT)

The Proposal

Malachi, one of the last prophets of Israel before Christ's birth, rebukes the Jews for doubting the Lord's promises and compares their unfaithfulness to the breaking of marriage vows. In this illustration, Malachi underscores the importance of spiritual oneness in marriage when he says, "Guard yourself in your SPIRIT and do not break faith with the wife of your youth." (Malachi 2:15)

The significance of spiritual harmony in marriage is so important that Malachi repeats the warning in verse 16 to "guard yourself in your spirit" so that you don't break the bond between you and your spouse. Spiritual oneness is the foundation that every other area of your marriage is built upon.

THE EXAMPLE

Some couples begin their journey in two completely different spiritual camps: an atheist married to a Christian; a Unitarian married to a Baptist; a Buddhist married to a Catholic; a Yogi married to a Jew. More often than not, couples on drastically different mystical quests find themselves facing difficult spiritual obstacles and startled by the dissent that follows. And if they do manage to live amicably, their spiritual journeys will likely take them in separate directions.

Other partners begin their relationship in the same spiritual camp: they're both Christians, for example, or perhaps they're both on a spiritual quest and have, at the very least, made a pact to look for answers in the same places, together. These couples—and likely their family and friends—are usually surprised by any spiritual division flowing from what appears to be such a united front.

As mentioned in the Welcome section, true "oneness" requires intentional pursuit and mindfulness. When pursuing and building spiritual oneness in particular, one must also, as Malachi encourages, take great care to "guard" the spirit in the process.

Note that to guard something means to stand watch over it and protect it in order to keep it safe. Therefore, to guard our spirits in a marriage means to be quite intentional about how we cultivate not only *our* souls, but also how we maintain a safe place that nurtures and encourages the spiritual growth of our spouse as well.

Spiritual Oneness

A pastor we knew long ago used the description of a "spiritual triangle" to explain that by focusing on growing closer to Jesus we could, at the same time, grow spiritually more intimate with one another. Picture it with us: at the top of the triangle is Jesus, and at each point of the base of the triangle is the husband and wife, respectively.

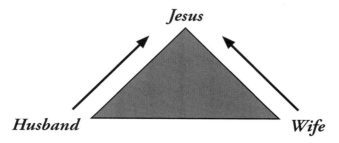

If *both* the husband *and* the wife pursue Jesus at the top of the triangle, then, inevitably, the spouses will grow closer to one another as well, in essence tightening up the triangle and developing a spiritually deeper connection. If each spouse fiercely and intentionally guards the other's efforts toward spiritual enrichment and Christian growth, then they will grow *toward* one another in spiritual intimacy. The endgame? Spiritual oneness.

Naturally, both the husband and the wife will likely move at different paces; the husband may encounter a grand spiritual breakthrough drawing him closer to Christ while the wife simultaneously experiences a spiritual dry spell, or vice versa. But no matter: as long as the couple commits to the pursuit of drawing close to Jesus (and thus, inevitably toward one another), then neither breakthrough nor barrier will keep them from growing in spiritual oneness.

Theoretically, guarding one another's efforts toward spiritual enrichment and Christian growth sounds wonderful, but practically, what might that look like in a real-life marriage? Here is a list of ways spouses can encourage one another to move toward Jesus:

- Study the Bible—together, with friends, with your children, individually

- Pray—for one another, together, with friends, individually

- Discuss with one another what God is teaching and revealing to you

- Lead or participate in a small group at church together

- Conduct family devotions together—either formally or informally

- Work on memorizing the same Bible verses throughout the week or month

- Encourage your spouse to meet regularly with an accountability partner

- Promote your spouse's connection with more mature Christian friends

- Support your spouse's investment in the lives of younger believers

✓ • Listen to and share Christian music with one another

✓ • Worship together

✓ • Attend church together

- Go to conferences together and/or make it possible for your spouse to attend Christian conferences with other believers

- Minister to others together

The bottom line is this: spiritual oneness isn't just going to happen. Each spouse must make deliberate decisions that foster movement toward Jesus which will, in turn, strengthen the spiritual oneness between husband and wife in marriage.

ONE-ON-ONE

1. What do you do daily/weekly/monthly to further your spiritual walk?

   Pray + meditate
   relisten to sermons around church / scripture
   listen to Christian music + devotionals
   church
   (read Bible)
   ask others advice
   + learn from other books
   Christian author @ church
   serve + out
   Pray
   listen to Worship music
   church
   (read Bible)
   Serve @ church + out

2. Share how each of you can assist the other in nurturing your time with God. Be as specific as possible and don't be afraid to share your spiritual struggles.

   StoK *Lead family more intentionally — daily | deep | devotionals ?*
   Find small group as family weekly Again

   KtoS *Ask me weekly about quiet x's / readings*
   Help me find good kids Bible Study to do w/ girls
   Find a small group

3. Jointly, come up with at least one activity that you can do together to enhance your spiritual relationship with each other (see the list in the previous section for ideas).

   Family devos
   Small Group

DATE NIGHT

Search for a Christian concert, worship night at a local church, or marriage conference in your area and attend it with your spouse. Need some more time to recharge or want to add some intimacy to your time together? Expand your date night over a couple of days or over a weekend, and use that time to plan how you are going to grow together spiritually.

The goal of this date night is to find an event or activity that will nurture both of you spiritually. After the event, discuss how you can create more time in your schedules to add spiritual growth opportunities that you can enjoy together.

OUR STORY:
PURSUING SPIRITUAL ONENESS

WE BEGAN OUR MARRIAGE UNIFIED IN SPIRITUAL PURPOSE. By that, we mean to say that we were both believers, confessing that Jesus is Lord and believing in our hearts that God raised Him from the dead (see Romans 10:9). In other words, we had the same basic spiritual beliefs and were, thus, in the same spiritual camp.

Coming out of a pretty rebellious lifestyle that involved quite a lot of drinking and subsequent poor decision-making that ended an intense college relationship, I (Rhonda) was delighted to find Mitchell, a Christian who kept me on the straight and narrow. In my mind, I had struck relational gold! He was a Christian; I was a Christian, and thus, ¡Voila! Spiritual oneness! (Or so we both thought.)

It didn't take us long to realize that while we did hold the same basic beliefs, we didn't necessarily have the same idea as to how to best grow—and grow *together*—in our spiritual pursuits. As you can imagine, this caused quite a bit of tension early on in our relationship. In short, simply being in the same spiritual camp does *not* automatically equal spiritual oneness.

Lesson Two:
Physical Oneness

KEY VERSE

Do you not know that your body is a temple of the Holy Spirit...?
Therefore, honor God with your bodies.
~1 Corinthians 6:19, 20

THE PROPOSAL

PAUL WAS THE SPIRITUAL FATHER of the church in Corinth, and as such, the church desired Paul to address several conduct issues that had arisen. In chapter 6, Paul confronts the problem of sexual immorality within the church and explains that what we do with our bodies directly impacts our relationship with Christ since it is His Spirit that lives within us.

The instruction we are given by Paul to "honor God" with our bodies is not specific to only sexual conduct, but all conduct. With regard to our body, the Bible tells us to be disciplined (1 Corinthians 9:27), modest (1 Timothy 2:9), self-controlled (Matthew 5:29), and sober (Ephesians 5:18) while warning us of over-eating (Proverbs 23:21), and laziness (2 Thessalonians 3:10). Physical oneness comes when a couple holds each other accountable in how they use their bodies.

✝ THE EXAMPLE

Paul referred to the body as the "temple" of the Holy Spirit, and therefore we should take care in how we treat it. Of course, this includes how we behave sexually. Paul says in 1 Corinthians 6:18 that we should "flee from sexual immorality. Every other sin a person commits is outside the body, but the sexually immoral person sins against his own body."

Therefore, if we truly hope to achieve physical oneness in marriage, we must understand that choosing to "sin against" our own bodies means sinning against our spouse as well. That said, "fleeing from sexual immorality" is essential to achieving physical oneness in our marriages. But what does that mean? Obviously, that means keeping sexual interactions within the bounds of our Biblically-defined marital relationship (see Matthew 19:4-5 and Hebrews 13:4).

Sexual oneness in our marriages is important—so important that we're devoting an entire section to it (see Lesson 5), but as mentioned in "The Proposal" above, physical oneness encompasses more than sex.

For example, if we overeat or drink excessively or if we under eat or exercise abusively, then we are treating our own body with contempt. And because married life by definition means we share our body with our spouse, then disrespecting our body really amounts to disrespecting our spouse.

Becoming physically one with our spouse requires vulnerability. It means having potentially difficult conversations where spouses tell of their innermost struggles with weight or food, addiction or abuse, exercise or pain—anything that may literally affect the flesh, and therefore their physical well-being.

The bottom line is this: when one spouse's physical well-being weakens, the other's physical sense rises to the occasion. A spouse may need extra care or assistance, for example, or require an accountability partner to change dietary habits. Perhaps he or she will want help with developing an exercise plan, or desire company when incorporating various changes in his/her lifestyle. Whatever the case, a husband and wife seeking physical oneness will strive not only to be attuned to the physical well-being of the other, but also to step up to the plate to help each other through any physical weakness.

ONE-ON-ONE

1. What areas of your life need improvement with regard to honoring God with your body? (As you are listening to your spouse share, remember that this can be a vulnerable process so take care to create an environment that is not overly critical or judgmental.)

2. How would you like to be held accountable in those areas? How can your spouse help you with this accountability? (Again, accountability is not a license to be critical. It should be seen as a supportive measure that helps your spouse grow and if/when there is failure, it is a safe place to confess that shortcoming.)

3. Write down 2-3 goals based upon your answer in #1 and next to those goals suggest ways to celebrate when those goals are met. Whether it's losing weight (lost 5 pounds this month!), going sober (no alcohol this week!), or exercising (ran 2 miles today!) make sure you create small enough goals so that you are celebrating often. This will help keep you motivated!

DATE NIGHT

For this date night, you and your spouse are going outdoors. Choose a day or evening when the weather is forecasted to be nice and commit to spending 1-3 hours doing something active. If you live in a warm climate, go walking, swimming, or hiking. If it's cold outside, you can choose ice skating, cross-country skiing, or snow shoeing. Don't have the right equipment or have never done the activity before? Perfect! Rent the equipment and try something new.

The goal of this date night is to establish a physical activity that you can enjoy together. Once you establish an activity you both enjoy, try to incorporate it into your life. Make time to enjoy being active together. Spending time in this fashion not only helps you stay healthy but also builds in time for conversation and connection.

Lesson Three:
Emotional Oneness

KEY VERSE

*We will speak the truth in love, growing in every
way more and more like Christ.*
~Ephesians 4:15 (NLT)

THE PROPOSAL

HOW WE COMMUNICATE with our spouse will build the emotional
bridge of trust on which our relationship will rise and fall. In his letter
to the Ephesians, Paul reminds us that it is not only *what* words we
use but also *how* we use those words that can either build up or tear
down communication between two people. In marriage we can get
overly comfortable with our spouse by delivering truth in its rawest,
harshest form—at times even using it as a weapon.

It's clear in scripture that Paul urges us to be honest with each other but in a way that encourages and builds up one another. The result? An emotional bond that not only draws us closer to each other but also closer to Christ.

THE EXAMPLE

In his book *The Listening Life,* Adam S. McHugh describes listening as a "profound act of hospitality" where we invite another person into our space in order to hear all they have to say. An important aspect of this listening is that we provide a secure space for the other person to be heard. The concept applies well to marriage: spouses should be acutely aware of welcoming each other into the safety and warmth of generous reception to exchange innermost thoughts and feelings, questions and fears, struggles and temptations.

If we're not careful, however, we'll offer kindnesses of time and geniality more and more to others, and less and less to our spouse. Familiarity with one another in the marital covenant develops such a high level of comfort that we may slowly begin to forgo the pleasantries of hospitality toward one another, replacing them with second-rate bits and scraps of attention making it nearly impossible to share deep-seated intricacies of the heart.

Worse, we may come to believe that our covenantal love and closeness grants us license to catapult hard truths at the other forgetting that Paul said to speak the truth *in love* to another and not merely to speak the truth just *because* you love each other. Marriage, perhaps more than any other relationship, should be the place most sheltered and out of harm's way where a person is welcomed into the private, gracious sorting out of heart issues. Unfortunately, the opposite is often the case.

In his book *Social*, psychologist Matthew D. Lieberman explains that, "In Eastern cultures, it is generally accepted that only by being sensitive to what others are thinking and doing can we successfully *harmonize* with one another so that we can achieve more together than we can as individuals." In fact, his examination of research in social neuroscience indicates that our need to connect with other people is more basic than our need for food or shelter. It follows, then, that if we refuse to pursue and build emotional oneness with our spouse, we will seek emotional connectedness elsewhere.

That said, if we want to be undivided emotionally with our spouse, we'll fling (even the legitimate) excuses aside to invite our spouse once again into the sanctuary where we contemplate our innermost thoughts. Consider these hard questions, for example:

- Are there too many activities on my calendar to connect— really connect—with my spouse? If yes, then it's time to reprioritize the appointment book.

- Does my extreme extroversion require the attainment and maintenance of so many relationships that my introverted spouse has been relegated to the bottom of the list? If yes, then it's time to reprioritize the social calendar, putting my hard-to-connect-with spouse at the top.

- Is it safer for my spouse to share difficult truths with friends than it is to share them with me? If yes, then it's time I learn how to better create a safe haven for my spouse to come *to me,* to share *with me,* and to be heard *by me.*

undivided MARRIAGE

Pursuing and building emotional oneness could be some of the most harrowing and time-consuming work of your marriage, but the rewards and benefits contribute heavily to creating spouses who live undivided in their marital covenant.

ONE-ON-ONE

1. How do you feel you and your spouse deal with difficult issues or disagreements?

   Pretty bad. Snippy. Passive Agressive
   Ignore + hope they go away. Tell but hurt or offend
   Sometimes can talk thru well — have gotten better
   abt communicating over years.... or weve gotten
   better abt pushing each others buttons

2. What suggestions do you have for improving communication in your marriage?

   Remember this verse + live this
   verse out when talking.
   Talk in love + not exaggerate

3. In what area do you feel you need more support from your spouse?

   Actually talk + not shut down. Lead the
   conversation w/ biblical truths.

   W/ Empathy + more understanding + not be so
   definsive

DATE NIGHT

Spend a night in a cabin, go camping, or send the kids to grandma's house. Do whatever you need to do to eliminate distractions including modern-day temptations like television, phone, and the internet. It's time to connect like it's 1799.

The goal of this date night is to open up lines of communication. Setting the mood can be really important so light some candles, play some music, or do what's necessary to create a relaxing atmosphere.

Start with the following topics, and then feel free to add some of your own!

- Take turns telling the story of how you first met. (It's amazing, and sometimes funny, how different our stories can be about the same event!)

- Separately, tell the story of your wedding day from the moment you got out of bed to the moment you crawled back in bed that night.

- Describe what your perfect day with your spouse would look like. Where would you go? What would you do? How would it end?

- Tell each other about your greatest fear and why it scares you. If it's an issue that brings about frequent anxiety, discuss ways you can help each other in this area.

- Discuss one situation in your marriage that you wish you could "snap your fingers" and change instantaneously. Realizing that change takes time and patience, discuss with your spouse the steps you need to put in place to accomplish the desired outcome.

- If you have young kids, grab a piece of paper and write down the answers to the following for each child: Between you and your spouse, to whom are they most similar in personality? When they grow up, what will be their profession? What type of person will they marry? How many kids will they have? What will be their biggest struggle in adulthood?

- Remember to add some of your own questions to this list. If there's something you've been waiting for the "right time" to discuss—now's the time!

Lesson Four:
Intellectual Oneness

KEY VERSE

*Be like-minded, be sympathetic, love one another,
be compassionate and humble.*
~1 Peter 3:8

THE PROPOSAL

AS WE HAVE DISCUSSED up to this point, God desires us to be of one flesh in body and spirit. Now, Peter, writing specifically to husbands and wives in verses 1-7, says we should also be of one mind. Just as communication is key to building emotional bridges with our spouse, intellectual stimulation in marriage is key to building like-mindedness.

This doesn't mean we have to agree on everything, but rather we should be "like-minded" in our pursuit of God-honoring decisions.

Our intellects need to be on the same page in wanting to put God first in our marriage. At the end of verse eight, Peter ends his list with the word "humble." If we are truly of one mind, then we will put ourselves last so that God can be first.

The Example

The very word "intellectual" might be intimidating to some, especially when pursuing intellectual oneness with another person. Perhaps you don't feel particularly intellectual, as in intelligent or well-educated, academic or bookish, knowledgeable or sophisticated; in short, you may not consider yourself to be all that "brainy." Or perhaps, when thinking about your marriage, you find that you represent the literary, cerebral type, while your spouse personifies experiential, hands-on characteristics.

No matter your level of intellectual capability (or your spouse's), Peter calls all believers to champion a likemindedness with one another. Pursuing intellectual oneness in our marriage, then, is less about achieving scholarly goals and more about a simple sharing with one another our thought-life, including what we're learning, how we're being challenged, and that with which we may be wrestling.

It's important to identify what intellectual oneness is not. Chasing after mental oneness does not mean that both husband and wife must hold the same opinions on every topic from the menial (what color shall we paint the kitchen?) to the practical (in what location does it make best sense to build our home?) to the theological (what does Scripture say about the end times?). It does mean that when differences arise in any area of thinking, we strive to achieve a harmony of thought—a likemindedness—that promotes God-honoring decision-making and peacefulness in our home.

Intellectual Oneness

The truth is that when any two people join together in marriage, they are bringing to the table many differences. Pursuing intellectual oneness, then, does not mean hammering out these differences to reach a cookie-cutter sameness in thought. Instead, it means being vulnerable enough to share innermost thinking always with the intent to end discussion in peace just as Paul, in his final greetings, exhorts fellow believers to "encourage one another, be of one mind, live in peace." (2 Corinthians 13:11)

While it is important to have the same mindset regarding the deep essentials such as beliefs about Jesus and salvation and morality, it certainly doesn't mean that a couple's gifts and habits and tastes must match. Mike Mason, in his book *The Mystery of Marriage*, says,

> True oneness is distinguished less by its sameness than by its differences. One partner is a man, the other a woman, and that's just the beginning. One is sociable, the other reclusive; one likes a down quilt for sleeping, the other a light blanket—and only half a light blanket at that! How can two such opposites ever be one? Might as well ask how a glove fits a hand. Oneness arises from differences fitting together, from contrasts corresponding.

Oneness arises from differences fitting together, from contrasts corresponding.

God sees, knows, and loves the differences in both you and your spouse, and in fact, He grows and teaches and challenges each of you in a way that is tailored perfectly for each of your personalities—personalities He designed. That said, humbly sharing with one another how God is growing and teaching and challenging you will inevitably draw both of you together intellectually as you pursue Him.

ONE-ON-ONE

1. How, where, and when do you and your spouse most often share your thoughts and feelings with each other? What, if anything, would you like to change that might be helpful to improve the frequency and quality of your sharing time?

2. When disagreements occur with your spouse, how do you pursue "likemindedness"? What challenges do you face in your relationship that may prevent you and your spouse from pursuing a God-honoring resolution?

3. Share with your spouse a moment in your marriage when you felt the two of you were most vulnerable with each other. What happened to create that vulnerability? Who initiated the conversation? How did your spouse react? How can you create more opportunities to be vulnerable with each other?

DATE NIGHT

The goal of this date night is to learn (or re-learn) how to be vulnerable with your spouse, and there's no better way to do that than over dessert! Go to your favorite restaurant for ice cream, cake, pie, or other sweet treat and make sure you bring paper and pens/pencils.

At some point during the date, take two pieces of paper and (separately) create a "same" column and a "different" column. Now, write down ways you and your spouse are the same and ways you are different. Share your lists with each other and discuss the following questions:

- What "same" qualities work to your marriage's benefit? Why?

- What "different" qualities work to your marriage's benefit? Why?

- Are there any qualities on your lists that are the cause of frequent disagreements? If so, discuss what needs to happen for those qualities to benefit your marriage rather than be a stumbling block.

OUR STORY:
PURSUING INTELLECTUAL ONENESS

MITCHELL AND I ARE WILDLY DIFFERENT in so many ways: he is introverted, I'm extroverted; he is extremely self-disciplined, I'm a little more loosey-goosey; he learns by research, I learn by doing; he is great with numbers and technology and music, I like words and books and podcasts; he is a planner, I am more spontaneous; he is a realist, I'm an idealist; he lives in the future, I live in the now.

Initially, these differences attracted us to one another, but over time, they were a source of conflict. For example, going on vacation for me meant picking a place and taking off to explore it; for him, it meant researching, calendarizing, and planning. By the time he was ready to go, I was bored and on to the next thing. He felt under-appreciated; I felt over-scheduled.

But over time, we have been intentional about identifying, understanding, and embracing our differences. Not only that, but our respective differences have sparked personal growth in one another. My extroversion encourages him to be more social; his self-discipline inspires me to become more self-controlled; my ability to live in the present has helped him to enjoy the now; his realism grounds me and gives traction to my idealistic notions. Our differences still cause quarrels now and then, but ultimately, understanding how to make them work together grows us toward a likeminded, team approach to marriage.

Lesson Five:
Sexual Oneness

KEY VERSE

The wife's body does not belong to her alone but also to her husband. In the same way, the husband's body does not belong to him alone but also to his wife.
~1 Corinthians 7:4

THE PROPOSAL

IN PAUL'S LETTER TO THE CORINTHIANS, he was writing to believers against a backdrop of carnal worship and sexual immorality. Corinth's infamous temple dedicated to Aphrodite, the Greek goddess of love, dominated the city's culture and dictated its sexual "norms" of practicing religious prostitution.

Paul brings clarity to the discussion of sex when he unequivocally states that sexual relationships are reserved for a wife and her husband because "sexual immorality is occurring." (1 Corinthians 7:2) He further states in verses 3-5 that in marriage, our bodies are not our own. They belong to our spouse; and therefore, we should not withhold sex from one another. In essence, sexual oneness occurs when we think of our bodies as not our own.

THE EXAMPLE

If we aren't careful, our "me first" culture that reveres and advocates for the relentless pursuit of "my" dreams, "my" desires and "my" needs will reduce sexual intimacy in marriage to a personal craving rather than a holy, unifying necessity.

That's right, sex in marriage is a *necessity*—not *just* for the man or *just* for the woman—but for the unity of the couple. We propose that both the frequency of physical intimacy and the feelings about it can be likened to the gauges on a vehicle: they predict whether or not something is wrong under the hood of our marriage. Gary Thomas, in his book *Sacred Influence,* suggests that "sexual desire can knit a man to a woman, or Satan can use it to build an ever-growing reliance outside the home." If, then, we are serious about building a marriage that will remain undivided, we must be very thoughtful about addressing sexual desire—or lack thereof—in the bedroom.

To be fair, the obstacles preventing intimacy in our homes are many. Do any of these sound familiar?

The kids are still awake. We just can't until they're sound asleep.

The walls are so thin… what if someone hears us?

Now that the kids are in bed, I really need to finish this project.

I'm so very tired. How about tomorrow?

I have a headache—for real!

I'm kind of annoyed at you, and so I don't feel like it.

Each of these hinderances is valid; however, we need to remove these snags preventing us from sexually connecting or they'll grow into a real barrier between husband and wife. And couples who aren't connecting sexually may be tempted to satisfy that desire elsewhere—perhaps through pornography or adultery.

"The monstrosity of sexual intercourse outside marriage," says C.S. Lewis in *Mere Christianity*, "is that those who indulge in it are trying to isolate one kind of union (the sexual) from all the other kinds of union which were intended to go along with it and make up the total union." Couples intent on becoming one flesh seek to have unity in every area of their relationship, so to look for any other kind of union (be it sexual or emotional, intellectual or spiritual, etc.) with anyone other than our spouse causes dire discord.

However, the Bible does single sex out as having a special impact on our efforts to become one flesh. Paul states it this way in 1 Corinthians 6:16-18:

> There's more to sex than mere skin on skin. Sex is as much spiritual mystery as physical fact. As written in Scripture, 'The two become one.' Since we want to become spiritually one with the Master, we must not pursue the kind of sex

that avoids commitment and intimacy, leaving us more lonely than ever—the kind of sex that can never 'become one.' There is a sense in which sexual sins are different from all others. In sexual sin we violate the sacredness of our own bodies, these bodies that were made for God-given and God-modeled love, for 'becoming one' with another." (from Eugene Peterson's *The Message)*

Made for "God-given and God-modeled love, for 'becoming one' with another," our bodies are not just meant to connect physically. Something more—something mystical—happens when husbands and wives make love. Like Paul says, sex is a "spiritual mystery" that makes us to "become one flesh," perhaps in a manner unlike any other activity in which we engage.

ONE-ON-ONE

Talking about sex is not a straightforward endeavor. Past sexual history, sexual abuse, and other factors can impact how sex is perceived. The following questions do not attempt to tackle deeper sexual issues that may be prevalent in your marriage. We would encourage you and your spouse to seek professional Christian counseling to address those matters.

1. How would you define the sexual health of your marriage? Discuss your different points of view and share with your spouse ways YOU are willing to change to make sex better for your spouse.

2. What does having sex communicate to you? In other words, what message is sent when your spouse wants to have sex with you? Explain why this is important to you.

3. What are the common barriers in your marriage that prevent you and your spouse from having sex? How can you overcome them in the future?

DATE NIGHT

There should be no guessing where this date night is going to lead! Clear your schedule, send the kids to grandma's, and book a room at a hotel in your favorite destination city—or simply stay at home for the night. Feel free to extend this date night over the entire weekend if you desire.

Too often we have feelings we don't verbalize which can lead to resentment, anxiety, and even anger. This occurs far too often in our marriages when it comes to talking about sex. As your spouse is sharing, remember that s/he is emotionally exposed and vulnerable.

The success of this date night depends on encouraging emotional honesty while responding to each other with love.

Start the night by expressing what you find attractive about each other. Nothing is too shallow and nothing is too deep.

Talk with your spouse about sexual frequency. Share your "ideal" number of days per week with your spouse, and if your numbers vary greatly, discuss how to resolve or compromise the differences.

Ask your spouse what s/he likes about your current sex life. Be specific (this is where the vulnerability begins!). Are there things you would like your spouse to do more often or perhaps less? Are there times of the day, settings, or even smells that are more conducive for you to be interested in sex?

Next, ask your spouse if there's anything you currently don't do during sex that s/he would like to try. Remember, 1st Corinthians 10:23: "Everything is permissible, but not everything is beneficial. Everything is permissible, but not everything is edifying." (Berean Study Bible) Also, don't forget that this lesson is entitled "Sexual Oneness." Being united in your sexual life is more important than any one person's desire.

Finally, you have the whole night alone…take advantage of it and have fun!

Lesson Six:
Moral Oneness

KEY VERSE

For it is from within, out of a person's heart,
that evil thoughts come.
~Mark 7:21

THE PROPOSAL

IN THE GOSPEL OF MARK, another confrontation between Jesus and the Pharisees is recorded in chapter seven. The Pharisees, always trying to discredit Jesus, want to know why his disciples are eating with defiled (unwashed) hands. Jesus gives a scathing retort ending in verse fifteen with, "Nothing outside a person can defile them by going into them. Rather, it is what comes out of a person that defiles them."

Using the imagery God gives us of being "one flesh," we also would have "one heart" in our marriage. If either spouse corrupts that heart, the other spouse is not immune to the damage done. The actions of one spouse impact the other. Therefore, we must protect our marriages from moral failure whether it comes through the tongue (gossip, slander), the mind (coveting), or the body (sexual immorality, gluttony).

✠ THE EXAMPLE

At its most basic core, morality is typically defined as a set of principles that help navigate the differences between right and wrong; it's a system of beliefs upon which to define the distinctions between good and bad behavior. The question, then, is this: from where do you and your spouse get the principles and beliefs that guide you to right and good conduct?

Ravi Zacharias says, "Pure morality points you to the purest one of all. When impure, it points you to yourself. The purer your habits, the closer to God you will come. Moralizing from impure motives takes you away from God" (from *The Grand Weaver: How God Shapes Us Through the Events of Our Lives*). Thinking back to the "spiritual triangle" in Lesson One on spiritual oneness, it follows that if *both* husband and wife pursue what Zacharias says is "pure morality," then they will *both* draw closer to God. As both draw closer to God, they'll inevitably draw closer to one another.

In order to pursue this "pure morality" of which Zacharias speaks, spouses must be intentional about reading, studying, and applying God's Word. The writer of Hebrews indicates that "the word of God is alive and active. Sharper than any double-edged sword, it penetrates even to dividing soul and spirit, joints and marrow; it judges the thoughts and attitudes of the heart." (Hebrews 4:12) God uses His Word, then, to "penetrate" us to the soul; through it, He "judges" the thoughts and attitudes of our hearts. If we want to get morally sound instruction, spending time in the Bible is a must.

You may read these words and lament that perhaps either you, your spouse, or both of you lack in the area of Bible study. Well, there is no time like the present to get started. God says about His Word that "it will not return to me empty, but will accomplish what I desire and achieve the purpose for which I sent it." (Isaiah 55:11) Another version says it like this: "I send [my Word] out, and it always produces fruit. It will accomplish all I want it to, and it will prosper everywhere I send it." (NLT) God's Word always produces fruit— *always*. Whether you or your spouse are seasoned studiers of Scripture or not, you can trust that He will work in and through your every attempt at delving into His Word.

Pastor, teacher, and author Watchman Nee warns that "the character of the world is morally different from the Spirit-imparted life we have received from God" (from *Love Not the World)*. That said, neglecting the wisdom of Scripture as we establish our moral compasses is to open our marriages up to the unreliably fickle and constantly changing moral whims of the world—a world very much different from the "Spirit-imparted life we have received from God."

The bottom line is this: if we want to strive toward moral oneness in our marriage, our morality must be informed, defined, and shaped by the same time-tested and trusted source: God and His Word.

undivided MARRIAGE

ONE-ON-ONE

1. How often do you read or discuss Scripture together? How do you think you could best improve this area of your marriage?

2. In what areas of your life do you feel most morally vulnerable (lust, gossip, dishonesty, greed, etc)? How can your spouse help you maintain your moral integrity in those areas?

3. Where have you seen God do His greatest work in your life? Where has He redeemed you? How did this happen?

DATE NIGHT

This date night actually occurs in the morning. Plan to have breakfast with your spouse when you have a few hours to spend time together without distractions. Maybe you stay home and fix a hearty breakfast of your own while giving the kids unexpected permission to watch a movie in the other room, or maybe you go to your favorite diner together and order the farmer's breakfast special.

The goal of this date night is to spend time in the Word together. Read Ruth chapter 2 & 4 and learn of the courtship and marriage of Ruth and Boaz. Then, answer and discuss the following questions: What first attracted Boaz to Ruth? How did faithfulness play a role in the relationship? How did Ruth and Boaz serve each other in their relationship? What can you learn from this love story that might improve your marriage?

Lesson Seven:
Financial Oneness

KEY VERSE

Every city or household divided against itself will not stand.
~Matthew 12:25

THE PROPOSAL

THESE WORDS WERE SPOKEN BY JESUS in response to the Pharisees who had accused him of driving out demons in the name of Satan. Because Jesus' opponents could no longer deny his miraculous powers, they resorted to charging him with sorcery—a capital offense punishable by death. Jesus essentially responds by saying that those who work against themselves cannot survive.

Statistically, finances rank as one of the top reasons for divorce. In marriage, we cannot remain as one if we are divided. Financially living as one requires us to bring everything to the full knowledge of the other. That means no secret checking accounts and no hidden drawer of cash. We must discuss and agree on how we use the resources God has given us. We must work together and respect one another so that we stand as one… lest we fall divided.

✝ THE EXAMPLE

While both Christian and secular financial management gurus agree in many areas when it comes to money management, there is one area where stark division prevails: whether or not couples should maintain joint or separate checking/savings accounts.

Writer Heather Koerner wonders in her *Boundless.Org* article "The Two Shall Become One… Checkbook" why there is such a disparity between secular and Christian financial advisors when it comes to marital checking/savings accounts. After much digging, she proposes "that it's not just about the accounts. It's about what each group believes about marriage—what marriage is and how to make it work well."

Popular personal-finance expert Suze Orman, for example, when giving marriage advice to a 25-year-old woman on Oprah Winfrey's Web site, said, "You love this guy, yet you're smart enough to hold on to your identity… I want you to have both a joint and a separate one [account]. The former ensures that you're protected as a couple; the latter is where you find the certainty that you'll never be dependent on somebody else."

Orman's advice in a nutshell is that the couple should develop a financial life specifically ensuring both husband and wife can dabble a bit in oneness (with a joint account) while at the same time cultivating and maintaining independence (with separate accounts). Her main objective for the wife is that she "never be dependent on somebody else."

Contrast Orman's advice with the guidance of Howard Dayton (a Christian) in his book *Money & Marriage God's Way*. After reminding readers that "they are no longer two, but one flesh" (according to Matthew 19:6), Dayton explains that in marriage "independence decreases; interdependence increases."

Did you catch that? *Interdependence increases.* In a culture that idolizes independence and individuality, the very idea of choosing to become more and more *interdependent* with a spouse is, in and of itself, counter-cultural. If our goal in marriage is to become one, however, then we must strive to become one in the area of finances even if it's not culturally popular.

But what does it look like to achieve financial oneness? It means there is no "mine" and "yours" when it comes to money; there is only "ours." It means there is no "my decision" or "your decision" when it comes to financial choices; there is only "our decision."

Renowned financial counselor Larry Burkett has said, "Money is either the best or the worst area of communication in our marriages." How would you describe communication in your marriage when it comes to money? If you would say your communication is strong, ¡Bravo! Praise God! Keep up the good work! If it's in need of some improvement, then consider this an area to grow together in love and trust—an area in which you can gain ground in becoming a couple *undivided*.

ONE-ON-ONE

1. If you are not sharing your financial resources completely, what is the reason for not doing so? What areas of distrust must be overcome? What will it take for you and your spouse to be "financially one?"

2. How are financial decisions made in your marriage? Is there discussion prior to purchases outside the budget? Do you establish a budget together? If not, why?

3. What do you think is the greatest financial challenge facing your marriage? Discuss together how those challenges will be met and what must be done to overcome them.

DATE NIGHT

The purpose of this date night is to talk about…money. If your first instinct is to skip this date, then this may be the date night you really need! Financial oneness doesn't happen without being intentional about it.

The location for this date night is up to you. You may want to stay at home, go to your favorite diner, or make a picnic and go to a park. Just make sure you choose an environment with minimal distractions.

As you begin, discuss with your spouse if you would like to have more (or less) involvement in the family finances. This is an opportunity for both of you to share whether you feel overburdened or uninformed about what happens with your money.

Next, discuss the "Big 3" financial pillars of marriage:

1. **Budget**

   - Do you have one? If not, pledge to get a good workbook on budgeting from Crown Financial Ministries or search for a local Financial Peace class at an area church.

   - Is your current budget accomplishing what you want it to? Are you saving enough? Paying off debt fast enough? What are the goals that you want to accomplish by having a budget?

2. **Debt**

   - How much do you have? Total all the debt you have and write down the number. Include mortgage, cars, credit cards, etc. How does that number make you feel?

- Next, determine when you would like to be debt free (in 10, 20, 30 years)? Now, figure out how you are going to accomplish that goal. Increase your mortgage or car payments? Pay off your credit card bills? How is that going to impact your budget? What sacrifices will need to be made? Note: Giving should never be an option when choosing an area of your budget to sacrifice. God asks that we give out of our "firstfruits" (Proverbs 3:9) which means giving should be a priority in our budget.

3. **Savings/Retirement**

- Do you have a "rainy day" fund for emergencies? If you lost your job, could you live 3? 6? 9? months off your savings? Are you saving separately for big purchases such as a car or house so that you can minimize your debt? Should you use some of your current savings to pay off debt?

- What is your plan for your post-working years? What are your goals financially for that time in your life? Even if your 30+ years away from that time in your life, it's to your advantage to discuss those goals now. The sooner you begin planning and saving for your post-working years, the easier it will be to accomplish your financial goals.

Lesson Eight:
Parental Oneness

KEY VERSE

My child, listen when your father corrects you.
Don't neglect your mother's instruction.
~Proverbs 1:8 (NLT)

THE PROPOSAL

THE BIBLE MAKES IT CLEAR that parenting is a two person job. The roles indicated in Proverbs 1:8 are not exclusive to each parent (some translations attribute "instruction" to the father and "teaching" to the mother). The wisdom shared in this verse, however, is that as parents, we work together to raise our children.

But as parents, what should our goal be? Where do we start and what is the end game? Ephesians 6:4 says our parenting goal should be to "bring them up in the discipline and instruction of the Lord."

The original Greek used for the word "discipline" is *paideia* which means "the whole training and education" of our children. The implied meaning is that parents are responsible for the cultivation of a child's mind and morals in addition to teaching kids to respect and care for their bodies.

THE EXAMPLE

Turn on just about any family comedy, and it won't be long before a variation of the following scenario unfolds: a child goes to his mother and asks if he can go to his friend's house; Mom says no. A few minutes later, that same child goes to his father with the same request; Dad says yes. Having successfully pitted mom against dad, the boy skips off to the neighbor's house leaving the parents wondering what just happened.

Unfortunately, scenarios such as this are not just relegated to TV sitcoms. All too often, one parent takes on the role of "bad guy" (the parent who always says no) while the other parent plays the part of "good guy" (the parent who always says yes). Children pick up on this dynamic and cunningly pit one parent against another. Division between mom and dad might be funny on TV, but a divided family in real life is no picnic.

It's common advice to encourage struggling parents to "get on the same page" in their parenting strategies, but what does it really look like to present a united front when teaching, training, and disciplining children together? In her book, *Team Us*, Ashleigh Slater writes about her wedding day saying, "When I walked down that aisle, I was a 'me.' When Ted and I walked back up it, that "me" had become part of 'us'—Team Us, as I like to call this new formation."

Parental Oneness

While it is natural for a mother and father to divide and conquer all the tasks associated with parenting—tasks such as meal-making, tooth-brushing, calendar-keeping, kid-bathing, house-cleaning, chore-assigning, toilet-training, homework-helping, clothes-shopping, Bible-teaching (and much more!)—we must take care that in the division of tasks, we aren't inadvertently dividing into separate sides. We must remember that we are on the same team—Team Us, as Ashleigh describes—growing children *together*.

That means that if mom says "no" to Junior, Junior automatically knows that dad is going to say "no," too, and vice versa. In fact, if mom says "no," Junior isn't even going to *approach* dad about the topic because he knows that when one member of the team speaks, the whole team speaks.

A united front does not come naturally, however. Both spouses must work hard to develop a parenting game plan for Team Us. It will require many, *many* private strategy-setting discussions. For example, who will take the lead on discipline issues and when? What shall be the consequences when children are disrespectful? What if we disagree on a parenting issue that comes up? For each family, strategy discussion topics will vary, but the most important tactic of all is that the husband and wife make time in private to design a single, united parenting plan.

Henry Ford said, "Coming together is a start. Keeping together is progress. Working together is success." As parents, we must make time for the coming together and the keeping together so that we can have the success of the working together. That said, one of the biggest deterrents of unity in parenting—and in family unity as a whole—is an over-booked calendar. If you or your spouse harbor anxiety at the thought of adding the ever-important task of making and keeping an ongoing parenting strategy session, it might be time to pull back on activities.

In *The Lifegiving Home: Creating a Place of Belonging and Becoming,* Sally Clarkson says, "All people need a place where their roots can grow deep and they always feel like they belong and have a loving refuge. And all people need a place that gives wings to their dreams, nurturing possibilities of who they might become." When we become couples who make time to pursue parenting oneness in our marriages, our homes become that place where our kids' roots grow deep with a sense of belonging, where their dreams are nourished, and where their futures are shaped.

How would each of you describe your home life (a direct fruit of parenting oneness) right now? Do you feel that you're on the same page when it comes to rearing your children in the way they should go? Do you feel that your family is not only fed, but also mentally, physically, emotionally, and spiritually warmed, safe, and nourished in your home? If your answer is "no" to any of these questions, then now is the time to clear some time on your calendar to have a strategy session with your spouse; it's time to tighten up your team tactics for your marriage, for your kids, for your family.

Pursuing parenting oneness is no easy task. But the benefits can impact the world. "What can you do to promote world peace?" asked Nobel Peace Prize Winner, Mother Teresa. "Go home and love your family." Be encouraged; what you, mom and dad, do now may impact the world!

ONE-ON-ONE

1. Describe to each other your parenting goals. How do your goals differ? How do they complement each other? What areas of parenting need to be addressed so you and your spouse are on the "same page" regarding your parenting strategies?

2. In what ways are you educating your child(ren) morally and spiritually? What can you do to be more intentional about teaching your children God's word?

3. How do you think you can be a better parent? How can your spouse be helpful in that pursuit?

DATE NIGHT

As you are working your way through this devotional, your kids may feel a little left out as you schedule date night after date night. Well, not this time! For this date night, the kids are included.

Before you embark on your family date night, gather the kids together and briefly explain why you and your spouse have been reading this marriage devotional and that tonight, your date night includes them. The goal of sharing with your children is so they understand that your marriage, your relationship, is a priority. It's another opportunity to educate your kids that marriage is not a one time "act" but a process that deserves your time and attention.

Next, have all the ingredients you need to make pizza. Include your kids' favorite ingredients as well as yours. Make sure everyone participates in the making of the pizzas. Take this opportunity to share stories about your relationship with your spouse. Children are always interested in who you were and what you did before you became parents. Choose a few good stories from when you dated, talk about your wedding day, and include each child's birth story. Anything you think might be interesting, share it!

Once the pizzas are done, it's time to break out the family movie. You can either pre-select a movie or have a few movies available and let your kids choose. Then, enjoy your time together as a family and remember that your children were a big reason you chose to spend the rest of your life with your spouse.

Lesson Nine:
Vocational Oneness

KEY VERSE

You did not choose me, but I chose you and appointed you so that
you might go and bear fruit—fruit that will last.
~John 15:16

THE PROPOSAL

OUR MODERN DAY DEFINITION of vocation usually focuses on finding
a job or career. However, the Latin root, and early definition, of the
word really means "calling." John says in verse 16 that we were chosen
or called by God. As a couple, we may have different jobs but what is
our joint calling? For what purpose has God drawn us together?

Clearly God views married couples as a single entity ("one flesh"),
so when God says, "I know the plans I have for you" in Jeremiah
29:11, we need to ask ourselves—do we know the plans God has

for us as a couple? What is our marital vocation (calling)? Earnestly pursuing the answer to this question can energize, revitalize, and revolutionize your marriage.

THE EXAMPLE

Jesus taught that we should "seek the Kingdom of God above all else, and live righteously, and he will give you everything that you need." (Matthew 6:33 NLT) In his blog post entitled "Got Mission," author and speaker Gary Thomas expounds on what this verse can mean for married couples when he points out what Jesus is *not* saying in this passage: "We're not told to seek first an intimate marriage, a happy life, obedient children, or anything else. Jesus tells us to seek first one thing, and one thing only: His Kingdom and His righteousness (the two words define and build on each other, creating one common pursuit)."

So often, a husband and a wife become so intensely focused on their individual jobs (whether those jobs are in the home or outside of it) that they're slowly drawn apart by separate ambitions. Of course it is not always feasible for spouses to intertwine their individual career paths into a single intimate pursuit, but it *is* possible for a couple to maintain separate professions while at the same time adhering to an overarching marital mission—a "higher calling," if you will.

For example, American writer and theologian Frederick Buechner said in his book *Wishful Thinking: A Theological ABC* that "vocation is the place where our deep gladness meets the world's deep need." What a beautiful definition of "vocation." As a couple, then, the question becomes (as mentioned earlier): What is our marital vocation? What is our calling as a couple?

Vocational Oneness

The possibilities are literally endless! We know one couple who does full-time medical missionary work together in the mountains of Peru; another couple who blogs/writes/speaks as advocates for the family in our culture; and another couple who, early on, pledged that their home would be a "lighthouse" in their neighborhood, and to that end they routinely host family-friendly get-togethers that promote rich community and fun fellowship as a backdrop for sharing Christ with people who live in their sub-division.

Your marital mission could be something that impacts a tight circle of influence such as becoming foster parents, looking in on senior citizens in your neighborhood, or signing up to be a Sunday school teaching duo at your church. Or your marital mission could be something that affects a larger population such as recording and promoting Gospel-centered YouTube videos, supporting a Christian church in a Third World country, or setting up a non-profit organization that supports fledgling Christian artists. Further, your marital mission may look like one of you taking the lead role (maybe you're the writer, the speaker, the spokesperson), and the other occupying the support position (maybe your spouse is the accountant, the business mind, the receptionist, the "worker bee", the videographer).

Whether your mission impacts large or small, whether you are the headliner or the support—the most important step toward vocational oneness in your marriage is to "join around a common aim" and "begin taking steps to move toward it," says Gary Thomas. "...as long as you're both aligned and committed, that's all it takes to join yourselves into a common task. Such a connection bolsters intimacy, meaning, and purpose."

And ultimately, isn't that what we all want in our marriages? More intimacy? More meaning? More purpose? Pursuing vocational oneness can bring you that and more!

undivided MARRIAGE

ONE-ON-ONE

1. What do you think your "calling" is as a couple? If you and your spouse are not certain of your calling, be sure to take time to discuss thoroughly all your possibilities.

2. When have you seen God use your marriage to impact other people's lives? What is preventing you and your spouse from being used in the same way again?

3. How might your friends describe the impact you and your spouse—as a couple—have on other friends, on the community, or at church? You may want to ask several close friends what they perceive your marital mission to be. Do you think their answers are accurate? If not, why aren't they seeing your marriage in the same way you do?

DATE NIGHT

On this date night you are going to discuss your marital vocation by watching a movie and having dinner together (ideally in that order).

You can choose any type of movie, rented or in theaters, action or rom-com, or maybe even a YouTube documentary. Look for an inspirational story where the main character faces great odds that seem too big to overcome or accomplish by him/herself.

After your movie, choose a restaurant (or take-out/delivery) and make sure you have an atmosphere conducive for talking. Discuss what you found inspiring about the movie. How did the main character find his/her purpose? What decisions did s/he have to make to overcome obstacles to accomplish his/her mission?

Now, it's time to discover your own marital vocation! Answer the following questions separately. Jot down key words and phrases to your answers and save for the next section of questions.

1. What energizes you?

2. When you are at the end of your life, what are two or three things you don't want to regret not doing?

3. What would make you wake up in the morning excited about your day?

4. Is there an activity you currently do where you lose track of time each time you do it?

5. What things outside your family do you value most?

Next, discuss those areas where you may have overlapping interests.

1. Are you both energized by the same type of activities?

2. Do either of you have any similar fears or regrets?

3. Is there an activity you currently do together that excites you more than doing it separately?

4. What values do you have that overlap?

Once you identify areas that overlap, discuss whether or not you feel your marriage should be focusing more on those areas and less on others (e.g. commitments that drain you, activities that don't share your values, etc). This may mean small life-change like rearranging your schedules, or it may mean big life-change such as quitting your jobs. It's important to understand, though, that a small adjustment here and there is no less important than a large-scale, whole-life redesign.

Remember, God brought you together for a purpose. Some couples are just nearer (small change) to their purpose than others (big change).

OUR STORY:
PURSUING VOCATIONAL ONENESS

I (Mitchell) spent a good deal of of my 20s and 30s working my way up the corporate ladder from marketing manager to director, then vice president to president of various performing arts organizations across the nation. As is often the case, reaching the top of my profession did not provide the joy and satisfaction I had anticipated.

Struggling to reconcile my gifts and training with wanting to find a purpose greater than myself, I came home for lunch one day and told Rhonda that God was challenging me to trust Him with my significance and security and take a step of faith that I had been unwilling to take up to that point in my life. Not coincidentally, she picked up her prayer journal from that morning and showed me that she had been praying for that exact same thing!

Through a relationship with my friend Robert, I was aware of a tremendous need in pediatric assistive devices. Children whose lives could be dramatically changed with these devices were unable to get them due to a gap within the insurance system. After many discussions with Robert, I put together a business plan to start a nonprofit that would fill this gap in an effort to impact the lives of children and families across the country.

This is where my challenge to rely on God SOLELY and FULLY was put to the test. With Rhonda's support and encouragement, I quit my job and began assembling a national board of directors and medical council. Rhonda began writing grants while I focused on other fundraising efforts. In two short years, we raised nearly $1M dollars and gifted assistive medical equipment to families in over 25 states.

We look back on that time in our marriage as a time of tremendous growth both toward one another (as we worked together for a common cause) and toward God (as we relied on Him daily for direction and provision).

Lesson Ten:
Philanthropical Oneness

KEY VERSE

Whoever is generous to the poor lends to the Lord,
and he will repay him for his deed.
~Proverbs 19:17 (ESV)

THE PROPOSAL

AS DISCUSSED IN LESSON 7, money is often listed among the top reasons for marital strife. To restate Genesis 50:20, every good thing God created, the enemy works to pervert. Until we realize that we are stewards (not owners) of God's resources, we will be tempted by greed, and the resources given to us will be a constant stumbling block in our marriage.

How do we fight back? Generosity. "One gives freely, yet grows all the richer; another withholds what he should give, and only suffers want." (Proverbs 11:24 ESV) It is imperative that as a couple, we have a plan for giving—and giving generously. Marriages that revolve around generosity are often the ones most admired, and the ones that should be most emulated.

THE EXAMPLE

There have been entire books and even television documentaries devoted to defining the idea of philanthropy. Taking a look at the Greek roots of the word, however, a basic understanding of the concept could be described as love ("phil") of mankind ("anthropos"). Thus, anytime a person devotes time, talent, or treasure to an organization or a cause out of his or her love for mankind, one could be said to have engaged in philanthropy.

Being philanthropic in our marriage, then, sounds easy enough: we should simply find a worthy cause and donate hours, skills and/ or money. And for some, achieving philanthropic oneness is that effortless; but for many others, choosing together the who, what, when, where, and why of philanthropy is a little more complicated.

Why is pursuing philanthropic giving complicated? Because it means *taking* from the wealth of your own abundance—time, savings and expertise—and *giving* it away. The taking and giving away required for generosity sounds good on paper, but in reality, it's a little uncomfortable. It means sacrificing hours with your spouse or children; it means tightening the budget to plan for monetary generosity; it means devoting your abilities not just for the building of *your* marriage, home and family, but also for the needs of others.

64

Philanthropical Oneness

True philanthropy requires sacrifice. This is hard because we humans tend to live more on the selfish side—something Paul warns us about when he says "in the last days difficult times will come. For men will be lovers of self, lovers of money..." (2 Tim 3:1) We must be intentional in our marriages to thwart our tendencies toward selfishness and to run from our propensity toward greed.

Pursuing philanthropic giving together as a couple, then, helps us to obey Paul's command in Philippians 2:3-4 where he encourages us to "do nothing from selfishness or empty conceit, but with humility of mind regard one another as more important than yourselves; do not merely look out for your own personal interests, but also for the interests of others." Philanthropy does exactly that: it looks out for the interests of others, showing that we regard someone else as more important than ourselves. With the help of the Holy Spirit, we can overcome the obstacle of our selfishness to become generous givers, together.

Perhaps you and your spouse are not deterred by selfishness, and you very much want to live a life of generosity; however, you fear the toll that generosity will take on your own family and bank account. It's not that you don't want to be open-handed, it's just that you're afraid of the consequences. Ron Blue, founder of MasterYourMoney. com and president of Kingdom Advisors encourages us to remember that God owns all of our resources. In his book *Complete Guide to Faith-Based Family Finances*, he says, "If you really believe that God owns it all, then when you lose any possession, for whatever reason, your emotions may cry out, but your mind and spirit have not the slightest question as to the right of God to take whatever He wants, whenever He wants it. Really believing this also frees you to give generously of God's resources to God's purposes and His people."

To those still afraid to commit to giving resources away for the love of God and His kingdom: fear is a tool the enemy uses to stop you from doing exactly what it is that God wants you to do. Fear undermines our trust in God causing us to forget that He will take care of all our needs. Fear weakens faith.

Looking back over each chapter of this book, it is interesting to note that much of the subject matter culminates in this final topic of philanthropy. For example, drawing closer together spiritually, intellectually, morally, financially and vocationally all prepare us to look outside of ourselves to love others better. And that makes sense, doesn't it? The more time we invest in learning to love God and one another better, the more prepared we'll be to reach outside of ourselves to love God's people better, as well.

Paul said that "whoever sows sparingly will also reap sparingly, and whoever sows bountifully will also reap bountifully." (2 Corinthians 9:6) May we be a couple who is intentional about becoming not only one with another in our marriage, but also in becoming one with another as we steward our time, talent and treasure to bless those outside of our of marriages, too.

ONE-ON-ONE

1. How generous do you think you are with your time, money, and expertise? Why is it easy or difficult to give? Regarding time, money and expertise, which is easiest to give away and which is hardest? Why do you think that is?

2. In what areas of your life do you tend to be selfish? How do you think you can change those attitudes and how can your spouse be helpful to you?

3. How would you give away a million dollars? Where would you spend a whole week working for free? What talent do you possess that can be used for God that you currently aren't using?

DATE NIGHT

All the previous date nights have focused on you and your spouse. Now, it's time to focus on others. The goal of this date night is to become a "philanthropist" for a night.

Sit down with your spouse and determine the top 2 or 3 charitable organizations (don't forget your church!) about which you feel strongly. Then, research whether those organizations have an upcoming fundraiser, charity auction, or other event in which you could participate.

Next, schedule a date to attend the fundraiser and determine an amount with your spouse that you can give to support the organization. Challenge yourselves to give beyond what is "comfortable." After the event, discuss how you felt about giving beyond your comfort zone. Was there as much anxiety as you thought? Did it inspire you to give more? How much did it really affect your family budget?

As time passes, make sure you revisit this experience and discuss with your spouse how you can continue to plan for giving more. That might mean spending less, or it might mean raising more money through garage sales or a part-time job. Either way, see if you can make generosity a cornerstone of your marriage.

SPECIAL NOTE: If your favorite organization doesn't have an upcoming event, set up an appointment to talk with someone about the needs of the organization. Maybe you can help directly by giving of your time, talents or treasure, or maybe you can launch the organization's very first fundraising event and have a greater impact than you could ever have imagined!

In Closing

MARRIAGE IS HARD. Sometimes, really hard.

But you don't need anyone to tell you this, do you? From the moment the two of you walked down the aisle forever committing to the sentiment of "I do," it became clear that no shortage of stumbling blocks would mark your marital journey.

Most of us expect *external* difficulties—maybe the struggle to find fulfilling work or the inability to locate a home within the boundaries of the budget or the unforeseen necessity of caring for ailing parents. But for many, the *internal* struggles may be a harrowing surprise— disappointment in one another regarding spiritual growth or sexual connection, discovery of emotional brokenness or moral shortcomings, differences in intellectual interests or parental philosophies.

If we aren't careful, both the expected and unexpected strains will build barriers between us, and those barriers divide. But division is not God's heart for our marriages! From the very beginning, His plan was that "a man shall leave his father and his mother and hold fast to his wife, and they shall become one flesh." (Genesis 2:24 ESV)

Our hope and prayer is that this book inspires you to be intentional about drawing close to one another and developing the kind of intimacy God intended from the get-go. It's a beautiful truth that when TWO people strive toward becoming ONE flesh, they come closer to having the kind of marriage God intended all along—an *undivided marriage*.

About the Authors

HAVING BEEN MARRIED FOR OVER 25 YEARS, authors Mitchell & Rhonda Owens parent two girls: the oldest born on their 10th wedding anniversary and the youngest on their 20th. Mitchell is a pastor, high school tennis coach, and nonprofit CEO; Rhonda is a former high school English teacher, homeschooling mom and virtual assistant.

On any given day, the Owens family can be found exploring God's amazing world together, whether it's hiking through the mountains, snorkeling off a beach, or sailing across the sea.

Mitchell & Rhonda are the authors of the *Undivided* devotional series which can be found on Amazon, and they are also regular contributors to various blogs and websites. Follow Mitchell & Rhonda on Facebook (@mitchellandrhonda), Twitter (@mitchellsowens), or Instagram (@rhonda_owens, @mitchellsowens).

Made in the USA
San Bernardino, CA
13 October 2016